Handling information for l
disability workers

Series Editor: Lesley Barcham

Mandatory unit and Common Induction Standards titles

Communicating effectively with people with a learning disability
ISBN 978 0 85725 510 5

Personal development for learning disability workers ISBN 978 0 85725 609 6

Equality and inclusion for learning disability workers ISBN 978 0 85725 514 3

Duty of care for learning disability workers ISBN 978 0 85725 613 3

Principles of safeguarding and protection for learning disability workers
ISBN 978 0 85725 506 8

Person centred approaches when supporting people with a learning disability
ISBN 978 0 85725 625 6

The role of the learning disability worker ISBN 978 0 85725 637 9

Handling information for learning disability workers ISBN 978 0 85725 633 1

Handling information for learning disability workers

Lesley Barcham and Jackie Pountney

Supporting the level 2 and 3 Diplomas in
Health and Social Care (learning disability pathway)
and the Common Induction Standards

Acknowledgements

Photographs from www.thepowerofpositiveimages.com and www.careimages.com. Our thanks to Choices Housing for their help.

First published in 2011 jointly by Learning Matters Ltd and the British Institute of Learning Disabilities

British Library Cataloguing in Publication Data
A CIP record for this book is available from the British Library

ISBN: 978 0 85725 633 1

This book is also available in the following ebook formats:
Adobe ebook ISBN: 978 0 85725 635 5
ePUB ebook ISBN: 978 0 85725 634 8
Kindle ISBN: 978 0 85725 636 2

Cover design by Pentacor
Text design by Pentacor
Project Management by Deer Park Productions
Typeset by Pantek Arts Ltd, Maidstone
Printed and bound in Great Britain by Ashford Colour Press Ltd, Gosport, Hants

Learning Matters Ltd
20 Cathedral Yard
Exeter
EX1 1HB
Tel: 01392 215560
E-mail: info@learningmatters.co.uk
www.learningmatters.co.uk

BILD
Campion House
Green Street
Kidderminster
Worcestershire
DY10 1JL
Tel: 01562 723010
E-mail: enquiries@bild.org.uk
www.bild.org.uk

Contents

This book covers:

- Common Induction Standards – Standard 1 – Role of the health and social care worker

- Level 2 and Level 3 diploma units HSC 028 – Handle information in health and social care settings and HSC 038 – Promote good practice in handling information in health and social care settings

About the authors and the people who contributed to this book

Lesley Barcham

Lesley's career has been about learning. She trained as a teacher of deaf children in the 1970s and started out as a hearing therapist and then teacher of secondary aged deaf children. She has also worked in residential child care, as a teacher of children and adults with a learning disability in a further education college. Lesley gained a PhD from the Open University in the 1990s for her research into the development of education for disabled children in Southern Africa. Lesley has worked for BILD for 14 years on a variety of learning materials and programmes. From 2009 – 2011 she was seconded part time to the Valuing People Team as workforce adviser.

Jackie Pountney

Jackie has worked at BILD since 2004, where she supports organisations to offer learning disability qualifications to their staff. Before this she worked with people with learning disabilities, first with Birmingham social services department, and later in a further education college. She has co-authored 'Not behind the bikeshed' a resource pack for teaching health and personal education to people with learning disabilities, and was the author of the BILD publications *Your role as a learning disability worker* and *Protecting people who have a learning disability from abuse*.

Introduction

Who is this book for?

Handling Information for Learning Disability Workers is for you if you:

- have a new job working with people with learning disabilities with a support provider or as a personal assistant;

- are a more experienced worker who is studying for a qualification for your own professional development or are seeking more information to improve your practice;

- are a volunteer supporting people with a learning disability;

- are a manager in a service supporting people with a learning disability and you have training or supervisory responsibility for the induction of new workers and the continuous professional development of more experienced staff;

- are a direct payment or personal budget user and are planning the induction or training for your personal assistant.

Links to qualifications and the Common Induction Standards

This book gives you all the information you need to complete both one of the Common Induction Standards, and the unit on handling information for learning disability workers from the level 2 and level 3 diplomas in health and social care. You may use the learning from this unit in a number of ways:

- to help you complete the Common Induction Standards;

- to work towards a full qualification e.g. the level 2 or level 3 diploma in health and social care;

- as learning for the unit on handling information for learning disability workers for your professional development.

This unit is one of the mandatory units that everyone doing the full level 2 and level 3 diploma must study. Although anyone studying for the qualifications will find the book useful, it is particularly helpful for people who support a person with a learning disability. The messages and stories used in this book are from people with a learning disability, family carers and people working with them.

Links to assessment

If you are studying for this unit and want to gain accreditation towards a qualification, first of all you will need to make sure that you are registered with an awarding organisation who offers the qualification. Then you will need to provide a portfolio of evidence for assessment. The person responsible for training within your organisation will advise you about registering with an awarding organisation and give you information about the type of evidence you will need to provide for assessment. You can also get additional information from BILD. For more information about qualifications and assessment, please go to the BILD website: www.bild.org.uk/qualifications

How this book is organised

Generally each chapter covers one learning outcome from the qualification unit, and one of the Common Induction Standards. The learning outcomes covered are clearly highlighted at the beginning of each chapter. Each chapter starts with a story from a person with a learning disability or family carer or worker. This introduces the topic and is intended to help you think about the topic from their point of view. Each chapter contains:

Thinking points – to help you reflect on your practice;

Stories – examples of good support from people with learning disabilities and family carers;

Activities – for you to use to help you to think about your work with people with learning disabilities;

Key points – a summary of the main messages in that chapter;

References and where to go for more information – useful references to help further study.

At the end of the book there is:

A glossary – explaining specialist language in plain English;

An index – to help you look up a particular topic easily.

Study skills

Studying for a qualification can be very rewarding. However, it can be daunting if you have not studied for a long time, or are wondering how to fit your studies into an already busy life. The BILD website contains lots of advice to help you to study successfully, including information about effective reading, taking notes, organising your time, using the internet for research. For further information, go to www.bild.org.uk/qualifications

Chapter 1

Understanding requirements for handling information in health and social care settings

I just didn't realise how important reading and keeping good records was until I started to support Erica. When her support workers follow the information in her records she has a good day and keeps healthy. Following her detailed support plan around morning and evening care means that she starts and finishes the day well. Each day we write down what we have done and how things went. Because of Erica's medical needs we also keep daily records of her medication and seizures. This helps Erica, her mum, and the doctors notice any changes in her health. Erica keeps her own health records in her room for when she goes to the doctor's and also in case there is an emergency. We explain to her each day about the other records we fill in. Erica can see all of the records about her when she wants to; she has given permission for her mum to see most of the records too. We keep the records in a locked cabinet in the sleep-over room.

Janice – support worker

Introduction

Workers supporting people with a learning disability need to have excellent communication skills. As well as being good at verbal and non verbal communication you will also need to contribute to written communications such as records and reports. This is essential for all types of social care support. The type and extent of the record keeping required will depend on the kind of work you do, the way your service is run or whether you work as a personal assistant. If you work for a large organisation it is likely that you will be required to keep more records than if you are employed by an individual using a direct payment or personal budget. Certain records are mandatory for some types of service. This means that you are required by law to keep them. Some records relate only to the organisation or individual you work for. Whether you work for an organisation or an individual, you will be required to complete some written records as part of your work.

When handling information, it is important that you keep within the law and you follow the policies of your organisation. This will help you to protect the privacy of the people you support and their families. Storing information about people securely is essential in learning disability services.

Learning outcomes

This chapter will help you to:

- understand the types of information required when supporting people with a learning disability;

- explain the legislation and codes of practice that relate to handling information when supporting people with a learning disability;

- explain why it is important to have secure systems for recording and storing information when supporting people with a learning disability.

This chapter covers:

- Common Induction Standards – Standard 1 – Role of the health and social care worker: Learning Outcome 4.1

- Level 2 HSC 028 – Handle information in health and social care settings: Learning Outcomes 1 and 2

- Level 3 HSC 038 – Promote good practice in handling information in health and social care settings: Learning Outcome 1

Types of information required when supporting people with a learning disability

Most services which support people with a learning disability aim to give individuals more independence and control over their own lives. Many people with a learning disability are supported to develop their own person centred plans. Now it is commonplace for individuals to take an active part in meetings held about them or to chair the meeting. Many people hold information and records about themselves or have access to records held about them.

Many people develop their own person centred plan, inviting the people they want to be involved to their planning meetings.

In the not too distant past, records and reports were considered to be the property of the professionals who cared for the person. A vast amount of information was kept about people with a learning disability, and individuals and their families were not expected to read or have access to the information that was held about them. Nor were they expected to attend meetings where personal information about them was discussed and plans for their future were made. Nowadays, things are changing.

As you read this book about record keeping, and relate it to your own practice, it is important to bear in mind that the people you support should be as fully involved as possible in the record keeping process. This can mean:

- making records easier to read and understand;
- involving people with learning disabilities in report writing and record keeping where possible;
- checking that they are aware of the information held about them and why it is held.

For many people with a learning disability, family members are a constant source of love and support. Even if the person is now living away from the family home, their family will still be closely involved in their support. The records that your organisation holds about an individual belong to that person, and they need to give consent for others to see them. It is up to the person who they allow to access their records. The person with a learning disability you support may not want their family to see any records about their personal relationships, but be happy for their parents or an advocate to see their health records. For the person with a learning disability to be able to give consent they need to understand why the records are being kept, why they need to be held securely and the implications of sharing the information. If a person is unable to give consent for others to see their records then their family and an independent advocate should be included in making decisions about what would be in their best interests.

When a member of the family starts to be supported by the organisation, managers and support workers need to explain to family carers about the records and reports that are kept by the organisation and the measures that are taken to keep them secure. You need to provide this information in the most suitable format for the person, which could mean explaining it in a conversation, providing a leaflet, putting the information on a website or having information available in languages other than English.

Thinking point

Think about the records and reports that you have completed or contributed to in your work over the last two weeks. Why was the information collected? Was the person with a learning disability involved? How did it contribute to the person's support?

The records and reports kept when supporting people with a learning disability serve many purposes:

- They provide you with important and relevant background information about a person's life before you knew them.
- They tell you about the likes and dislikes, dreams and aspirations of the person you support.
- They help you keep track of events over a period of time.
- They help you to pass on information to other people.
- They help with planning staff working hours.

- They help to bridge gaps in knowledge between one person and another.
- They can show progress and development.
- They provide information about health issues.
- They detail how a person wants to be supported especially in relation to personal care.
- They document details about a particular incident or activity.
- They show how well a service is doing its job.

How involved you are with records and reports will depend on the type of work you do and where you work. If you work for a provider organisation you will probably be required to contribute to particular reports and records. If you work as a personal assistant, employed as part of a small team by one person to provide their support, the record keeping is likely to be just as important but could be less constrained by policies and procedures.

You may be surprised at the amount of record keeping that your job involves. However, records and reports are essential to good support. Keeping effective records and reports is key to ensuring that an individual with a learning disability is supported properly. Making records accessible to the people they are about is an important new challenge for social care workers and organisations.

Here is a list of written records kept by one organisation which supports people with a learning disability:

- initial assessments and history;
- day books or handover books;
- medical reports and medication records;
- accident records;
- personal finance records;
- bank account details;
- comments and complaints records;
- individual care plans or support plans;
- person centred plans;
- review reports;
- individual behavioural management plans;
- monitoring forms.

The organisation also keeps other records, such as risk assessments, safety records such as details about fire drills and fridge and freezer temperatures, staff rotas, reviews and appraisals and financial records. Some of these records relate to staff, some to the safety and protection of both staff and individuals with a learning disability and some ensure proper financial management. All are important in a high quality service.

Activity

Look at the list of records above and note down those that are kept by your organisation. Add to your list any other records that you are also required to keep.

Does the person you support have access to the records you have listed? If there are records the person does not have access to, talk to your line manager to find out why.

Legislation and codes of practice that relate to handling information in learning disability services

There are a number of laws, reports and codes of practice that you need to be aware of when handling information at work. These include the Human Rights Act, the Data Protection Act, the Caldicott Report and the Code of Practice for Social Care Workers. These guide organisations and individuals so that they can keep within the law and protect the privacy of the people they support and their families.

The Human Rights Act 2000

The Human Rights Act, Article 8, offers protection from interference by the state and public authorities into an individual's private and family life, home and correspondence. Public authorities include not only government departments, but also private and voluntary sector organisations carrying out functions of a public nature such as providing health and social care support. The holding, use or disclosure of personal information about someone is covered by Article 8.

Article 8 of the Human Rights Act is a qualified right. This means that interference by the state may be allowed under certain circumstances, for example:

- if it is in accordance with the law;
- if it is in the interest of protecting the health and rights of the person;
- if it is necessary in a democratic society.

The policies and procedures of your organisation will have taken account of the Human Rights Act and will give you guidance about when it might be permissible to provide personal information to others.

The Data Protection Act 1998

The Data Protection Act 1998 applies to the whole of the UK. It gives individuals certain rights about any information that is held about them, and it places obligations on those who hold and process the information. The Act applies to information held about you as a worker as well as to information about the people you support. There are eight principles of good practice that must be adhered to when handling information.

The principles of the Data Protection Act 1998

Data must be:

- fairly and lawfully processed;
- processed for limited purposes and not used for any other purpose than the one for which it was obtained;
- adequate, relevant and not excessive;
- accurate and up to date;
- kept no longer than necessary;
- processed in accordance with the individual's rights;

- secure;
- transferred to countries outside the European Economic Area only if that country has adequate protection for the individual.

The Caldicott Report

The Caldicott Report, written in 1997, sets out six general principles that the NHS Executive believes health and social care organisations should use when reviewing information held about the people who use their services. The principles describe how the confidentiality and security of personal information is maintained.

The Caldicott Principles

The following principles of good practice should be observed when handling information in health and social care settings:

1. A formal justification of purpose is required prior to sharing any information with others.
2. Identifiable information (about a particular person) is to be transferred only when absolutely necessary.
3. Information should be limited to the minimum required only.
4. Access to information should be on a need-to-know basis only.
5. All staff must understand their responsibilities in sharing information.
6. All staff should comply with and understand the law.

You will see that the Caldicott Principles link closely to the principles of the Data Protection Act, and together they give clear guidance about storing information within an organisation. During your induction you should be told about the data protection policies and procedures for your organisation. If you are a personal assistant you should also discuss this with your employer during your induction. Details about how you should contribute to and store personal information might be included in your contract of employment as a personal assistant.

Activity

Read through your organisation's policies and procedures on handling information. Can you see how the Caldicott Principles are included in the policies? Discuss your ideas with your line manager.

The Code of Practice for Social Care Workers

The General Social Care Council (GSCC) is the organisation set up by the government, in 2001, to register and regulate all social care workers in England. Similar bodies exist in Scotland, Wales and Northern Ireland (for details, see the references at the end of this chapter). Their Codes of Practice outline the standards that all social care workers should work towards. You should make sure you get a copy, read it and follow what it says about handling information and confidentiality. These are the standards that social care workers across the UK should be working to maintain.

The Code of Practice for Social Care Workers gives the following guidance for workers:

- You must strive to establish and maintain the trust and confidence of service users and carers. This includes respecting confidential information and clearly explaining agency policies about confidentiality to service users and carers.
- You must uphold public trust and confidence in social care services. In particular you must not abuse the trust of service users and carers or the access you have to personal information about them or to their property, home or workplace.
- You must maintain clear and accurate records as required by procedures established for your work.

You must maintain clear and accurate records as required by procedures established for your work.

By 2012 the functions of the GSCC will be transferred to the Health Professions Council, which will be given a new title to reflect its new responsibilities. You will need to look out for any material or guidance that is produced by this new organisation.

Why is it important to have secure systems for recording and storing information?

The information that your organisation holds about the people it supports and about its staff can be stored in a number of different ways, including in paper files and on electronic systems. All systems for storing personal information, for example names, addresses, telephone numbers, employment details, bank details, medical records and so on, must be operated according to the terms of the Data Protection Act. Organisations should have clear policies that show how they comply with the Act.

You will probably find that the following information is held on computer within your service:

- databases of information about people and organisations;
- people's names and addresses;
- individual assessments;
- records and reports of review procedures;
- medical records;
- financial accounts.

In addition, at least some of the following information may also be kept within your organisation, often in some type of manual storage systems:

- card indexes with factual information, like names and addresses;
- personal files – this information is stored in locked cabinets kept alphabetically or under different categories;
- record books or files with information on individual programmes and achievements;
- medical records;
- day books or handover records;
- personal financial records.

Most services have a formal policy on access to records. However, in practice the policy can be overlooked and workers may develop shortcuts to make it easier to get the information they need. This in turn can increase the chances of confidential information getting into the wrong hands.

For example, many of the records you will be dealing with will contain information that is personal and private. It's therefore essential to treat these records in a confidential way. This means that you only use the information in ways required by your employer – that is, in ways which are directly related to your job. You must not pass the information about an individual who uses your services on to anyone other than those who need it to do their job. Don't forget that confidentiality includes what you say to your family and friends at home or in the pub.

Practical ways to store and record information securely

Your everyday work will often mean you will need to record and store information securely. There are some practical steps you can take to maintain confidentiality in the way you handle this information.

General principles on recording and storing information:
- Respect confidences.
- Always assume that something personal is confidential unless the person concerned tells you otherwise.
- Help the people you support to understand what you can and cannot keep confidential.
- Do not make promises you cannot keep about keeping everything private.
- Discourage the people you support from giving you unnecessary personal or private information.
- Use the most private way possible to pass on private and personal information.

What to do when confidential information is written, passed on and stored manually:

- Do not leave personal files containing information anywhere that other people might be able to read or pick them up.
- Always put confidential papers away straight after using them.
- Lock files and cabinets that contain personal information.
- Make sure that if you take personal information from a filing system you put a note in the right place stating who has taken the file and when it was taken.
- Always ensure that you keep the information with you and never read it on public transport or leave it in your car.
- Anonymise any written material that is shared, for example in a training situation.

What to do when confidential information is stored electronically:

- Only use faxes or e-mails that are password protected or encrypted.
- Make sure you don't leave information on a computer screen open for all to see.
- Log off from a computer when you move away from the desk.
- Make sure, if you take electronically stored personal information about people away from your place of work, for example on a laptop or data stick, that you follow your organisation's policies and procedures on the safe storage of the equipment.
- Do not tell anyone your login details, such as your user name or password, and always change your password when you are asked to do so.

Activity

Think about the last four items of personal information that you handled at work. How did you make sure that the information was stored and used securely? Discuss your answer with your line manager at your next supervision. If you have any concerns about the safe storage of personal information discuss this with your line manager at the earliest opportunity.

Key points from this chapter

- Keeping effective records and reports is key to ensuring that an individual with a learning disability is supported properly.
- Confidentiality is an important part of being a learning disability worker.
- Assume all personal information is confidential unless you know otherwise.
- There are legal requirements relating to keeping personal information confidential. You must always work within the law.
- Passing on information without authorisation is against the rights of the individual. It shows a lack of respect for the privacy of the person you support and their family.
- Secure storage of manual information means putting files away immediately after use and locking cabinets that contain personal information.

- Secure storage of electronic information means logging off from a computer when you move away from your desk, not telling other people your login details and always following policies and procedures in the safe storage of information and equipment.

- Before you breach confidentiality always check your organisation's policy and with a senior colleague.

References and where to go for more information

References

Department for Constitutional Affairs (2006) *A Guide to the Human Rights Act 1998, Third Edition.* London: TSO

British Institute of Human Rights (2008) *Your Human Rights - A Guide for Disabled People.* London: BIHR

GSCC (2002) *Codes of Practice for Social Care Workers.* London: GSCC, downloadable from

- General Social Care Council (England)   www.gscc.org.uk
- Northern Ireland Social Care Council www.niscc.info
- Scottish Social Services Council www.sssc.uk.com
- Care Council for Wales www.ccwales.org.uk

Hughes, A and Coombs, P (2001) *Easy Guide to the Human Rights Act 1998.* Kidderminster: BILD

Legislation, policies and reports

Data Protection Act 1998
Department of Health (1997) The Caldicott Report. London: Department of Health
Human Rights Act 2000

Websites

Information Commissioner's Office (head office), for data protection information and for details about offices across the UK www.ico.gov.uk
BBC GCSE Bitesize Guide to the Data Protection Act www.bbc.co.uk
A guide to the Data Protection Act www.legislation.co.uk

Chapter 2

Maintaining records in line with agreed ways of working

I lost count of how many issues of verbal and physical abuse I reported. 'She's had an unsettled day' was the euphemism we had to use [in a report] for someone who'd been pinned to the floor.

Whistleblower Ashleigh Fox talking about the abuse at Winterbourne View, Sunday Mirror, 5 June 2011

There were deficiencies in record-keeping and in the planning of care.

Investigation into services for people with learning disabilities provided by Sutton and Merton Primary Care Trust (2007)

Workers' training records clearly demonstrate that they had all received the mandatory training and induction identified as required for the service.

Controlled drugs are being managed correctly; entries in the register demonstrate that named patient medication is being administered to the right person. The date, month and year are clearly recorded and two nurses were consistently signing the book.

Anonymised details from inspection reports

Introduction

As you can see from the quotes above, poor record keeping can be a contributory factor in the provision of poor support. Equally, good record keeping in relation to training and the management of medication can contribute to a safe service and to good outcomes for people. The quotes were taken from:

- a newspaper report about abuse in a learning disability secure hospital;

- an investigation into abuse in services in Sutton and Merton (2007);

- anonymised inspection reports of learning disability services.

In your work supporting people with a learning disability you have access to lots of information about them and their families that is highly personal. The way you deal with this information is extremely important. When you contribute to records and reports, what you write needs to be up to date, accurate and legible so that others can understand and act on what you have recorded.

You always need to act within the law and the Code of Practice for Social Care Workers, and to follow the ways of working agreed with your employer. If you work for an organisation, the agreed ways of working are more than likely set out in the policies and procedures. If you are a personal assistant then the agreed ways of working may be less formally documented. They may, for example, be set out in your contract of employment.

Learning outcomes

This chapter will help you to:

- know how to maintain records that are up to date, complete, accurate and legible;

- handle information in line with policies and procedures or agreed ways of working;

- describe how to access guidance, information and advice about handling information;

- explain what actions to take when there are concerns over the recording, storing or sharing of information.

This chapter covers:

- Common Induction Standards – Standard 1 – Role of the health and social care worker: Learning Outcome 4

- Level 2 HSC 028 – Handle information in health and social care settings: Learning Outcomes 2 and 3

- Level 3 HSC 038 – Promote good practice in handling information in health and social care settings: Learning Outcome 2

Maintaining records that are up to date, complete, accurate and legible

Before we look at how you can contribute to good record keeping, you need to consider how you will ensure that the people with a learning disability you support can contribute to and have access to their records. In many services today information is recorded in a format that is accessible to the person and it is their property. This doesn't mean that all organisations and all records are open and transparent and that there is equality in the collection and ownership of the information. But at least many organisations are making positive steps in this direction.

You need to consider how you will ensure that the people with a learning disability you support can contribute to and have access to their records.

When you are contributing to reports and records you need to keep in mind that you should:

- use all available opportunities to discuss the issues of record keeping with the people with a learning disability with whom you work;

- draw on your own knowledge and experience of joint record keeping and report writing with people with a learning disability when you are doing this activity;

- incorporate their perspectives into your thinking.

The difference between records and reports

Before going into the details about record keeping it is helpful to identify the difference between a record and a report. As a general rule, records are cumulative and ongoing, for example, a daily record of activities, medication taken, and progress in the new skills a person is learning. Reports, on the other hand, are written for a particular occasion or situation, such as a report of a meeting, an incident or accident, or for an annual review. Reports and records are different ways of recording information.

Records:

- often have a standard format, such as a form for you to fill in, questions for you to answer, or boxes in which to respond to certain questions;

- refer to information that is collected regularly or periodically, for example daily, weekly or annually;

- are used to record biographical information, numerical and/or statistical information such as personal contact details, medical information or attendance;

- are often used on a short term basis to monitor progress or developments, such as patterns of behaviour or the skills someone is learning.

Some of the information that might go on a form is constant, such as date of birth, details about certain medical conditions or syndromes. Some of the information that goes on a record will change – for example, monitoring information such as changes in health or behaviour, address and telephone numbers.

Reports:

- generally have a more specific purpose and relate to a particular event or situation, for example:

  - a report about a particular incident, such as an accident, or an event that happened unexpectedly with adverse consequences;

  - a report is more likely to relate to a particular event such as a review meeting, or when someone is transferred from one setting to another, or information is being given to family members or workers by a colleague from another organisation, such as a speech and language therapist or psychologist;

- a report is likely to be written in a more descriptive, narrative format. Some reports may need to follow certain guidelines or use particular headings, whilst others may be more freely written and the writer can devise their own structure and format.

Often information collected on records might help with writing a report. For example, when Joe's review meeting is due, Adam, his key worker, helps him prepare by looking through his health records and college reports. They show that his diabetes has been controlled better since he was prescribed the new medication three months ago and his weight loss has continued, although more slowly in the last six months. At college his reports indicate that he has achieved his customer service qualification and he has undertaken two work placements in local shops. The specific occasion or situation for which the report is being prepared is Joe's review meeting, but looking through past records and reports helps with this.

Similarly, if a crisis meeting is held because a woman supported to live in her own flat is experiencing serious problems, then the information is more likely to be written up as a report, rather than a record. This might include information on the person's recent health difficulties and the latest incidents with her neighbours. Having detailed reports about the recent verbal abuse that the tenant had been subjected to, together with her statements to the police, will help in compiling the report for the meeting.

Presenting information legibly and clearly

Thinking point

Have you ever tried to read something that is written in very untidy handwriting? How did it make you feel? Imagine you were at work and that you needed to access some information quickly, but it was illegible? What might the consequence be?

For some workers there are personal barriers to producing information. Not all of us have neat and easy to read handwriting, some of us need to work hard at making our handwriting legible. Some services require their staff to access, and complete, records or reports using computers, but not all workers are confident using a computer.

If you have problems that make it difficult for you to contribute to written records and reports you need to discuss this with your manager. There are a number of ways they might be able to assist you. Your employer may be able to help you to access IT, literacy, or English as a second language courses. For information about accessing support to develop your literacy and numeracy skills look in the *Personal Development for Learning Disability Workers* book in this series.

As well as making sure that any record or report you contribute to is legible, you also need to make sure that everything is clear to a potential future reader. This means not using jargon or abbreviations that someone reading the report might not understand. If you do need to use abbreviations or jargon, make sure you add a definition as well.

Presenting information that is accurate, complete and up to date

The information you record should be relevant, clear, concise and factually accurate. Look at the examples in the table below of information taken from records and reports.

What was written	What should have been written
Mickey was terrible at the centre, he had a bad session	Mickey sat in the corner for almost all of the drama session rocking and muttering to himself. He was sitting facing the wall and despite lots of encouragement from Aisha he only participated in the final ten minutes of singing time.
Alex was so horrible to Keith that Keith ended up going to his room	When Alex got home at 5.00pm from his day at the charity shop he started shouting at Keith saying, 'Loser, loser'. Keith's head dropped and he walked away. Alex did it again 3 more times in 15 minutes and Keith went to his room and slammed the door behind him.

Gurminder was sick all afternoon	Gurminder ate an egg sandwich, a banana and a cookie for lunch. She said she felt unwell half an hour after lunch and said her tummy hurt. She spent nearly an hour watching TV and dozing in the chair. After 3.00 pm she joined us in the garden and helped with weeding the tubs and watering the pots. She had no drinks or fruit at 4.00 pm with everyone else, saying she felt unwell. At dinner time she ate and drank everything, the sausages, mash and peas, the ice cream and fruit and she drank a glass of water and a mug of tea.

Different kinds of forms require different types of information. Sometimes it isn't easy to decide what to write and how much to write.

- Sometimes factual information is required, for example, why did Keith go to his room?

- Sometimes you need to make a judgement about a situation and then check this out, for example, why did Mickey behave as he did? Usually he really enjoys drama and joins in with everything.

- Sometimes you need to select and summarise information. Not everything that Gurminder did in the afternoon needs to be written down.

Here are some ideas for selecting and gathering information to ensure it is accurate and complete.

- Develop good observational skills to help you gather facts and assess situations. Note down the facts and not your opinions.

- Ask the person with a learning disability to tell you what they saw or heard to add to what you observed. You could ask Mickey why he sat in the corner at the drama session.

- Discuss events with colleagues or others who are close to the person, for example their family carer if they were involved in an event. Check out whether their observations are similar to yours.

- Ask yourself whether the information you select is needed for this particular purpose or whether it is irrelevant. For example, would it be helpful to add that Alex was involved in an argument with another volunteer at the charity shop that afternoon?
- Use other well written reports and records as examples. This means reports that:
  - are short and to the point;
  - give facts and not opinions, and don't have vague phrases such as 'had a bad day';
  - include the kind of information you and others need to do their work;
  - are written in the same way that you would want to see information written about yourself.

Activity

Rewrite the following examples so that they are clear, concise and factually accurate, including facts and not opinions.

- *Sally's language was really foul.*
- *Rachel loved the trip out with her family, and she was brilliant when she came back.*
- *All the staff did their mandatory training and really enjoyed it.*

Discuss with your manager or an experienced colleague, ask whether they agree with your changes.

Records and anti-discriminatory language

In the examples in the table above you probably noticed some examples of negative language, for example 'terrible' and 'horrible'. These words express negative judgements and might be seen as evidence of verbal abuse or discrimination on the basis of an individual's learning disability. Any negative judgements that are made in reports should be based on facts and not the personal opinion of the writer. All language used in reports should be factual and anti-discriminatory. When writing any report read it through and think about how you would feel if it was written about you or a member of your family. If you are unhappy with the language used or the content, it is more than likely that the person you are writing about or a member of their family would be unhappy with it as well.

It is important to sign and date records and reports.

Signing and dating records and reports

It is important to sign records and reports because signatures:

- tell you who to go to if you need more information;

- can help when organising activities, showing which staff work best with which person with a learning disability and who has had fewer opportunities to work with whom;

- indicate that you are doing a professional job.

It is important to date records and reports because dates:

- enable you to see whether something is still relevant today or if it is outdated;

- tell you how long something has been going on;

- help you to put things in sequence and follow progress;

- tell you whether records are up to date or have been neglected.

Remember that whenever you are involved in writing a report or record signing and dating the document is an important part of doing a professional job.

Handling information in line with policies and procedures or agreed ways of working

Activity

Find and read all the policies and procedures in your organisation that relate to handling information. This could include the policies on confidentiality, positive behaviour support, risk management, record keeping and data protection. When you have read them, see whether you can answer the following questions. Discuss your answers with your line manager.

1. *What are the procedures in your own service for reporting inappropriate breaches of confidentiality?*

2. *What must you do to ensure the security of manual and electronic records?*

3. *If you were asked for personal information about a person you support by someone from outside of your organisation what should you do?*

4. *What daily records should you be using and contributing to in your work?*

5. *A family carer asks to see the risk assessments completed with their son in relation to the adventure holiday he is going on next week. What should you do?*

If you are unsure about the answers to any of these questions you need to find out as soon as possible. If you cannot find the answer in the policies or procedures, then discuss them with your line manager or supervisor to make sure you understand your responsibilities. Once you have done this, try the activity again.

For more information about confidentiality, go to the *Communicating Effectively with People with a Learning Disability* book in this series.

All organisations have their own procedures in relation to confidential information, which employees are required to follow. However, some procedures are common across all organisations. These include:

- immediate action on the disclosure of inappropriate breaches of confidentiality, which involve dealing with the person responsible;

- disciplinary procedures, which vary according to the severity of the breach and which include verbal or written warnings that may be placed on record in the individual's personal file;

- some way of limiting the damage done;

- involving the person about whom the disclosures have been made.

In serious situations, it will be necessary to involve someone from outside the service, such as an inspector from the local authority or the regulatory body, or to contact the Information Commissioner's Office.

Accessing guidance, information and advice about handling information

Andrea had only been in her job for a few weeks when she took a call from the local hospital asking for information about Jamie, one of the men she supported. The person on the phone asked about his medical history and the medication he was taking. Andrea knew this information was private and she wasn't allowed to disclose it except in exceptional circumstances. If you were in the same situation as Andrea, what would you do? Where would you go for information or advice? Discuss your ideas with your line manager.

Whether you are new to supporting people with a learning disability or you are an experienced worker, there may be occasions when you are unsure about particular situations, for example whether to pass on information to colleagues, people from another organisation or a family carer. You may be asked to share information from records and reports with a person you support and they don't understand what has been written. In these situations you need to seek assistance.

You could get assistance about confidentiality and handling information from:

- the policies and procedures or agreed ways of working with your employer;
- your line manager or senior colleague or your employer if you work as a personal assistant;
- the data protection manager in your organisation;
- the Information Commissioner's Office www.ico.gov.uk

If you have concerns about record keeping and report writing identified in appraisal or supervision you can look for training opportunities, either provided by your organisation or by another provider such as the local college. Alternatively, you can ask an experienced colleague who is good at record keeping and report writing to provide on the job coaching.

Taking action when there are concerns over recording, storing or sharing information

In your work you may come across a number of concerns in relation to the recording, storing or sharing of information. These could include inaccurate, poorly completed records, lack of security in storing information, or a failure to involve people with a learning disability or their families in record keeping.

Activity

Read the examples below. If you were a support worker in these situations what would you do?

1. *All of the personal files for the people living in Nine Acre Home are kept locked away in the office, and none of the people living in the home have access to their records. Family carers are actively discouraged from reading the files of their relatives.*

2. *Luigi gives a copy of a confidential report to the manager of another service which also supports a person he works with. He doesn't ask the person first if he can share the report.*

3. *Billy's older sister wants to know how his money is being spent. Amy finds that there are no records for the past eight months to show how the money put into his account by the family has been spent. Billy's monthly statements from the bank are not in the right file. The earlier records are incomplete and haven't been signed or dated.*

4. *Alan is one of Aidan's personal assistants and he is concerned that when he starts work in the evening Aidan's medication records for that day have not been filled in. He doesn't know what medication Aidan has been given, when and by whom.*

If you have any concerns about poor record keeping or breaches of confidentiality then you should take the following actions:

- Discuss the matter, in confidence, with your line manager, or supervisor or your employer if you are a personal assistant.
- If no one is available and you feel the situation warrants immediate action, discuss it with another senior colleague.
- In serious situations, you may be required to make a written statement.
- You may also have to be available and prepared to make a statement at a later date if the matter warrants serious investigation.
- Where information is disclosed to an outside person or body, such as a relative or the press and there are adverse consequences like an assault or a newspaper story, you may be called upon to give evidence.

Key points from this chapter

- Keeping effective records is key to ensuring people with a learning disability get good support.
- The person you support should know about, be involved in, and have access to the records kept about them.
- Keeping clear and accurate records is an important part of your role as a learning disability worker.
- Different kinds of information require different structures and types of presentation.
- All recorded information should be presented clearly and should be understandable to the reader.
- Formal reports should be typed.
- Less formal records may be handwritten, but must always be legible.
- All records and reports should be signed and dated.
- Always avoid jargon or abbreviations. If you have to use them, explain them to your reader.

References and where to go for more information

References

Barcham, L (2011) *Personal Development for Learning Disability Workers.* Exeter: Learning Matters and BILD

Thurman S (2011) *Communicating Effectively with People with a Learning Disability.* Exeter: Learning Matters and BILD

Websites

Information Commissioner's Office (head office), for data protection information and for details about offices across the UK www.ico.gov.uk

Chapter 3

Supporting others to handle information

Joanne enjoys a busy social life and loves going out clothes shopping, dancing and to watch football. She has epilepsy, which is not always controlled by medication, and sometimes she has a seizure when she is out. Joanne knows that some people are scared when she has a fit and aren't sure what to do. She had a good idea, and asked me, her key worker, to develop an Easy Read information sheet with her, that describes what support she needs when having and recovering from a seizure. Joanne decides which of her friends to share this personal information with.

Geraldine – Joanne's key worker

Introduction

The records and reports that you contribute to as a learning disability worker are important to the person you support, their family members and to colleagues in your own organisation and others. In many situations you will need to work in partnership with others in either the collection of information, or its storage. Maintaining the security of our personal information is important to all of us and it is part of your role both to ensure the security of the information you use and also to explain to others how you and they can ensure the security of their information.

Supporting people with a learning disability to understand and contribute to records and reports challenges us to communicate effectively in a way that is comfortable to the person. This means providing information in a way that suits the individual's communication needs.

Helping people to understand the need for secure handling of information

Thinking point

How would you feel if you found out that your doctor or employer was keeping secret records about you? And that they were sharing them with other people without you knowing? How would you feel if your personal medical or employment records were discovered by strangers in a rubbish bin in a public place?

We all want to know about the records that are kept about us and we need to feel confident that these records are being held safely. One of the things you're likely to have to do, in the course of your work, is to help the person you support to understand about records, keeping information confidential and why it is important. Family carers, new colleagues from your own organisation and people from other organisations may also need to know about the records that you keep and how they are kept secure.

The kinds of situations in which you're likely to have to do this include:

- when you are reading or contributing to a person's records and you need to explain what you are doing to the person involved;

- when you are working with someone to produce a report and are collecting information from their records, for example for a review meeting;

- when the organisation you work for is going to be supporting a new person and you have been asked to explain to them and their family carers about the records that are kept and their security;

- if a difficult situation occurs in the service, such as financial abuse, and you need to share information with outside agencies, for example the police;

- if a person who uses the service overhears something confidential;

- when a person asks to see their records and reports but doesn't understand them because they are not accessible to them;

- if written information has been disclosed inappropriately and there are concerns about this.

There are a number of points you might need to discuss with people including:

- what information is held by the organisation about the people they support and why;

- the legal requirements about how the information is collected and stored;

- how the organisation puts their legal obligations into practice;

- whether the person is able to access the records kept about them;

- that the individual needs to give permission for their information to be shared with others, such as a family member, advocate or a person from another organisation such as a hospital or the police, except in a few exceptional situations;

- the procedure for sharing information with others should the person lack capacity to consent to it being shared;

- the organisation's policies and procedures on the secure handling of information;

- what the person should do if they have concerns about how information is collected and stored.

Activity

Think about one person that you support. What is their preferred communication method? How would you communicate with them about the need for the secure handling of information? Discuss your ideas with the person's key worker or your line manager. Do they agree with your ideas?

You need to be person centred in your approach to explaining about the secure handling of information.

When talking to people with a learning disability and others about records and reports and the secure handling of information, you need to be person centred in your approach. You should consider the communication method that the person is most comfortable with. People's communication needs can vary depending on any disabilities they might have, their first language and their life experience. You need to think carefully about the best way of providing information for the person, as not everyone likes to read policies and procedures. In fact, for many people with a learning disability, large amounts of detailed written information can be difficult for them to fully understand. When considering how best to pass on information you could think about:

- discussing the information in a one to one conversation, and planning the best time to do this;

- providing the information in a group setting, for example in a tenants' or residents' meeting;

- providing the information in a leaflet;

- making the information available as Easy Read (see page 36 for more information);

- having the information translated into the person's preferred or strongest language;

- making a short DVD or audio file.

When matching your approach to a person's ability, consider the following advice.

- Simplify the message, for example by 'translating' it in an appropriate way, as suggested in the section on translation on pages 33–37.

- Use real examples relating to the individual's own experience.

- Break your message down into manageable chunks which the person will be able to understand.

- Repeat as required and in context.

- Use other opportunities to get the message across.

- Reinforce positive responses, drawing the person's attention to the fact that they have kept the information confidential, so that they will realise what it means.

- It may be helpful to involve a relative, friend or advocate, so that the learning is reinforced and understood in different situations.

When supporting a family carer, friend, advocate or new colleague to understand about the secure handling of information, many of the above ideas about providing information for people with a learning disability also apply. Being person centred in your approach is important. You will find it helpful to identify the person's preferred communication method and their favoured learning style. Having information in a variety of formats to share with others is also helpful, such as in a leaflet, on a web page or in the form of information to share in a conversation.

Activity

Look back at the information about the Human Rights Act Article 8, the Data Protection Act and the Caldicott Principles on pages 6–8. Think of two ways that you could explain these to the person you thought about in the previous activity, or to their family carers. Discuss your ideas with your line manager or with colleagues at your next team meeting.

Thinking point

Look back over your work in the last two weeks. How did your actions demonstrate good practice in the secure handling of information? You need to show in your day to day actions that it is important to handle information securely and sensitively.

You need to show in your day to day action that it is important to handle information securely.

Supporting others to understand and contribute to records and reports

The fact that it is important to work in partnership with people with a learning disability in handling information doesn't necessarily mean that it is easy to do so. Undoubtedly, there are some people with a learning disability who are capable of taking control and of handling information in ways that best suit them, like Joanne in the example at the beginning of this chapter. But many people with a learning disability will require support of varying kinds to do this. This presents you with the challenge of finding ways of enabling them to play a full part in handling the information that relates to their own lives. This means that you need to think about different ways of 'translating' information so that the person can best understand it and make a contribution.

What is meant by translation?

Usually we think of translation as being from one language into another, for instance translating English into French or German. Indeed, in many parts of the UK, services are provided for people from a range of minority ethnic groups, so information must be made available in the appropriate languages if the services are to be open to all on an equal basis.

However, translation can also mean changing the form in which information is presented, for example:

- written information can be translated into Braille for blind people;

- spoken information can be translated into sign language for Deaf people;

- information can be translated into Makaton signs for people with a learning disability who either have a hearing loss or who have difficulty understanding or conversing in spoken language;

- information may also be presented in formats that are more understandable for people who have difficulty with literacy, such as symbols or pictures instead of words (which is often called Easy Read information);

- we might also translate complex language into simple language so that it can be more easily understood.

So the definition of 'translation' used in this book is much wider than the meaning we are accustomed to.

Why is translation important?

The main aim of all organisations should be to help people with a learning disability become empowered, autonomous and in control of their own lives. If we are to achieve this ambition, individuals within our services must have access to all information concerning them and must be in control of how this information is presented, disseminated and used.

Translation has a major part to play in this and is required in order to:

- ensure that people with a learning disability and, where appropriate, their relatives or other carers are at the centre of decisions concerning their lives;

- enable people with a learning disability to have access to documentation that has relevance for them, such as government papers, legislation and professional reports;

- make sure that they are partners in planning, providing and evaluating services;

- ensure that people with a learning disability and, where appropriate, their families have control over what is happening to them.

Why is translation needed in the following situations?

Susie is blind and has moderate learning disabilities. Before joining the day centre she now attends, she attended a special unit in a school for children and young people with visual impairments where she learned some Braille. None of the workers in the day service know Braille, so the only way information can be presented to Susie is orally.

This is unsatisfactory for various reasons. Susie, like the rest of us, can only remember so much of what is told to her verbally. She has no record of information presented and is not receiving information on an equal basis. She needs to have translation done by someone who can write Braille, so that she can participate fully in the activities of the service.

Sui Ling is Chinese and has profound and multiple learning disabilities. He is the only person in his day service from a minority ethnic background. The only member of his family who speaks any English is his ten-year-old brother. His brother is called on to translate things for his parents and to act as interpreter between the centre workers and the family.

This has many limitations: the brother often doesn't understand the intricacies of what is being said; his language and translation skills are probably not sufficient for the task; it places undue pressure upon him and it isn't appropriate to use a family member to discuss potentially confidential or sensitive information. In addition, Sui Ling is not involved, and it is his interests that are being discussed. The services of an independent adult translator are required.

Anna, the chair of the Residents' Committee, has a place on the management committee of a residential home. She receives the minutes and her support worker spends time going through them with her before the meeting.

The home is making an effort to include Anna, but there are still shortcomings. Anna will probably only remember a limited amount of what is told to her. Although she has her own copy of the minutes, she cannot use them or refer to them as other people can, which puts her at a disadvantage. She needs to have the minutes translated into a form she can understand, for example in an Easy Read version, if she can read or in picture or symbol format if this is more appropriate.

Translation can help with collecting and handling information and with other areas of consultation with people with a learning disability. Participation will be much more effective for people with a learning disability if information is presented in accessible formats. It will mean, for example:

- more effective consultation about service provision;
- better ways of enabling people to express their opinions, aspirations and needs;
- helping people to represent their own views and those of others they might represent;
- enabling people to pay a full part in meetings and discussions;
- finding better ways of developing true and equal partnerships;
- better joint planning;
- enabling people to play a full part on committees;
- meaningful participation and consultation;
- more opportunities for pursuing equal rights.

There are a number of practical books that can help you with making information accessible including, *How to make information accessible: Basic guidelines for people who commission Easy Read information* and *How to produce information in an accessible way.* For more information go to the reference section at the end of this chapter.

Different types of translation that might be required

There are many different ways of ensuring that information is accessible to people with a learning disability. These include:

- translation into a minority language, such as Urdu, Punjabi, Hindi, Arabic, Kurdish or Chinese;
- translation using symbols, such as Makaton symbols, or specific symbols devised by people with a learning disability themselves;
- translation of the written word into the spoken word, for instance where a supporter sits with the person with a learning disability, goes through the document and translates it into simpler language, checking back to see that the person has understood (although this method has its limitations – it can be time-consuming and tiring, it may be confusing for someone with a learning disability , the 'translator' is 'in charge' of what is selected, and it is difficult to retain large amounts of information presented verbally);

- translation from complex language and concepts and long sentences into simpler language and shorter sentences; this sometimes involves the production of two copies of a document, one in much simpler language;

- translation of text into pictures, either hand drawn or computer generated;

- translation of the written word into sign language, such as British Sign Language or Makaton;

- translation from written English into Braille for people with visual impairments;

- translation of spoken and written language into contact signing, such as that used by people who have both sight and hearing impairments;

- translation of information into specific signs, gestures and touch which are used by people with profound and multiple learning disabilities;

- producing information in other formats, such as video or audiotape;

- presentation of information on websites produced by and with people who have a learning disability, using formats which are appropriate, such as pictures, limited written information, large print, and good use of space.

Some general principles apply to all of the above situations:

- People with a learning disability will require more time to absorb information.

- Repetition is important.

- Information should be paced to suit the needs of the individual.

- If one method doesn't work, another should be tried.

These suggestions apply to the translation of information, in order to make it more accessible to people with a learning disability. However, they are also relevant to the collection of information by and with people who have learning disabilities and to the presentation of material collected by and with them.

Key points from this chapter

- There will be occasions when you will have to explain to a person with a learning disability, family carer or colleague about the need to handle information securely. You may need to explain:

  - that confidential information should be discussed in a private place;

  - their rights in relation to the private information held about them;

  - about the laws that set out how you must handle personal information;

  - how you and your colleagues ensure the security of their personal information;

  - that they have a right to see any records or reports about them;

  - what they should do if they have concerns about the information held about them.

- When supporting a person to contribute to information you need to find out about their preferred communication method.

- You may need to translate information for people if they have difficulty understanding spoken language, if they have a hearing or visual impairment, if they are from minority ethnic groups and have a first language other than English, or if the written materials are too formal and complex.

References and where to go for more information

References

CHANGE (2009) *How to make information accessible*, downloadable from www.changepeople.co.uk

DH (2009) *Basic guidelines for people who commission Easy Read information.* London: Department of Health, downloadable from www.dh.gov.uk

SCIE (2006) *How to produce information in an accessible way.* London: SCIE, downloadable from www.scie.org.uk

Glossary

Accessible information – information that people can understand. The information meets the person's communication needs. For example, this might mean providing printed information in the person's first language or in British Sign Language for a Deaf person.

Aims – a general statement of what an organisation hopes to achieve.

Code of practice – a UK document for social care workers setting out the standards they should be working to.

Confidentiality – things that need to be kept private.

Continuous professional development (CPD) – learning that you undertake after your induction that will help you develop in your role or that will advance your career.

Direct payments – a way for people to organise their own social care support by receiving funding direct from their council following an assessment of their needs.

Easy Read – information is sometimes called 'easier information' or 'simpler words and pictures'. It is a way of making information easier to read and understand for some people with a learning disability.

Family carer – a relative of a person with learning disabilities, who has an interest in their wellbeing.

General Social Care Council – the organisation that regulates the social care workforce in England and sets the standards of care through the Codes of Practice. In Scotland this is the **Scottish Social Services Council**; in Wales, the **Care Council for Wales/Cyngor Gofal Cymru**; and in Northern Ireland the **Northern Ireland Social Care Council**.

Induction – a period of learning, shortly after starting a new job or volunteering placement, when workers find out about how to provide good support to people with learning disabilities.

Jargon – technical language used within a particular profession or specialist area.

Job description – a document that gives detailed information about your work, what you will be doing, who you are responsible to, etc.

Person centred approach – a way of working every day with people with learning disabilities that puts the person and their dreams at the centre of everything you do.

Personal development plan – a plan completed by a worker with their manager to record their future learning and development needs.

Policy – a statement or plan of action that clearly sets out an organisation's position or approach on a particular issue and tells staff what should be done in the circumstances.

Procedure – a set of instructions which sets out in detail how a policy should be implemented and what staff should do in response to a specific situation.

Records – a way of collecting and storing information, often in a standard format such as a form for you to complete.

Reflection – careful consideration of ideas and issues.

Reports – generally written for a specific purpose, such as a review meeting, or can relate to a particular event such as an accident. Reports are likely to be written in a more descriptive, narrative format.

Rights – a framework of laws that protects people from harm, sets out what people can say and do and guarantees the right to a fair trial and other basic entitlements, such as the right to respect, equality, etc.

Service – the provision of social care support for a person, which could be in their own home, their local community, a residential home or similar place.

Support plan – a detailed plan of a person's support needs, which support workers should use to inform their day-to-day support for that individual.

Translation – changing the form in which information is presented so that it can be easily used.

Index

Added to a page number 'g' denotes glossary.

information storage 2
  concerns in relation to 25–6
  general principles 11–12
  guidance on 8
  systems 10–11
interference, protection from 7

J
jargon 39g
job description 39g

L
legible information, presenting 18–19
legislation 7–8

M
manual storage systems 10

N
negative language 21
Northern Ireland Social Care Council 39g

P
partnership working 28
person centred approach 31, 40g
person centred plans 2
personal assistants 8, 15
Personal Development for Learning
    Disability Workers 19
personal development plans 40g
personal information see information
policies and procedures
  access to records 11
  agreed ways of working 15
  confidential information 23
  data protection 8
  defined 40g
  disclosure of information 7
  information handling 22–3
  information storage 10
public authorities 7

Q
qualified rights 7

R
record keeping 5
  involvement of users in 3
  quality of support 14
  type and extent 1–2

recording information
  concerns in relation to 25–6
  general principles 11–12
records and reports
  access to 2, 3, 4, 11, 15
  defined 40g
  difference between 17–18
  importance 28
  involvement with 5
  maintaining 16–22
  purposes 4–5
  signing 22
  types 5–6
  user understanding and contribution to
      33–7
reflection 40g
reports see records and reports
rights 40g
  see also Human Rights Act
risk assessments 6

S
safety records 6
Scottish Social Services Council 39g
secure information systems 10–12
security of information 8, 28, 29–32
service 40g
signatures, on records and reports 22
social care councils 39g
support plans 40g

T
translation
  defined 33–4, 40g
  importance of 34–6
  situations requiring 35, 36
  types that might be required 36–7
trust 9

U
up-to-date information, presenting 19–21